zen-on score

KHACHATURIAN

"SPARTACUS"
SECOND SUITE FROM THE BALLET

Commentary by Koichi Owa

ex-VAAP AGENTS

●**Boosey & Hawkes Music Publishers Ltd.**
for the United Kingdom and British Commonwealth (except Canada)
and Republic of Ireland
●**Les Editions Le Chant du Monde, Paris**
pour la France, la Belgique, le Luxembourg,
l'Andorre et les Pays francophones de l'Afrique
●**Musikverlag Hans Sikorski, Hamburg**
für Deutschland, Dänemark, Griechenland, Island, Israel,
Niederlande, Norwegen, Portugal, Schweden,
Schweiz, Spanien und Türkei
●**Fennica Gehrman, Helsinki** for Finland
●**BMG Ricordi S. p. A., Milano** per Italia
●**G. Schirmer, Inc.**, New York
for the United States of America, Canada and Mexico
●**Universal Edition A.G., Wien**, für Österreich
●**Zen-On Music Co., Ltd., Tokyo**, for Japan

zen-on music

●

●

ハチャトゥリャン
バレエ音楽《スパルタクス》
第2組曲

解説　大輪公壱

アラム・イリイチ・ハチャトゥリャン（1903～1978）は、プロコフィエフやショスタコーヴィチ、またカバレフスキー等と並んで、20世紀ソヴィエト楽壇を代表する作曲家のひとりである。代表作は言うまでもなく、バレエ音楽《ガヤネー》（ガイーヌはフランス語読み）そして《スパルタクス》。付随音楽では《仮面舞踏会》、そして3つの交響曲は、中でも第2番「鐘」がよく知られている。また協奏曲の分野では、ピアノ及びヴァイオリンのためのものがその演奏頻度は最も高いと思われる。続いて作曲者の生い立ちを記してみよう――――。

ハチャトゥリャンは1903年コジョール村（グルジアのトビリシ市）に生れたアルメニア人である。そこはアルメニア、アゼルバイジャン、グルジアなどのいわゆる民族音楽の宝庫で、帝政ロシア時代から栄えた温泉保養地でもあった。

彼の父は製本業を営んでいたが、周囲の音楽環境には西洋のアカデミズム、すなわち18、19世紀ヨーロッパのクラシック音楽が満ちあふれていたとはいえハチャトゥリャンにとっての音楽との出会いは故国の民謡、民族音楽なのである。それは一生涯作曲者、その創作の根幹、いわば核となりつづけたものであったと言ってよい。彼はその‘音楽’との出会いを次の様に語っている。

「幼い頃、母はたいへん表情豊かにアルメニアやアゼルバイジャンの民謡をうたってくれた。そのひとつ、悲しい狩人のうたは、長い年月私の心に温められていて〈第2交響曲〉の第2楽章のテーマの基礎となった。音楽は街でも私を囲んでいた。グルジアの合唱、アゼルバイジャンの弦楽器のつまびきが聞こえてきたり、放浪の民族詩人・歌手のうたを何時間でも聴いた。幼い頃の私を包んでいた周囲の人々の音楽への情熱、音の形式、イントネーション、リズムなどは‘母乳’のように潜在意識の部分で私の作品にもしみ込んでいる。」「7歳の頃、民族音楽の魔力に本能的に引かれ、子どもなりに感嘆した。屋根裏部屋にこっそり忍び込み、いろんな物体をたたいて、立ち聞きして強い感動を受けた民族的なリズムを、さまざまな変化や組み合わせに努力しながら叩いてみたのを思い出す。こんな具合に私の最初の音楽活動は、私にとっては言葉に表せぬほどの楽しみであったが、それは私の両親を絶望におとしいれた――――」。

ハチャトゥリャンの両親はしかし、引っ越しの時、幸いにも前の居住者から安価にて古いピアノを買い取ることが出来た。

「私は、すぐさま民族的な歌や踊りのメロディーを、耳をたよりにさぐり弾きはじめた。説明しがたい満足感に満たされながら、私は１本か２本の指で際限もなく繰り返して棒暗記した―――」。これは作曲家寺原伸夫氏が師、ハチャトゥリャンから直接聞いた話である。（'民族音楽に囲まれて育つ' より寺原氏の文章を部分引用）［ビクター音楽産業のＣＤより］

1921年、18才のハチャトゥリャンは兄、スーレンとともにモスクワへ旅立った。グルジアにソヴィエト政権が確立された後のことである。彼は兄の忠告にしたがってモスクワ綜合大学生物学部の物理数学科の予科聴講生となるが、しかしこの時、ここで彼の生涯を決定した '音楽' との感動的な出会いが起こるのである―――。

「兄と二人で、たまたまモスクワ音楽院の前を通りかかり、コンサートがあるというので入ってみた。美しいホールには、大音楽家の肖像画が壁にかかげられていた。オーケストラはベートヴェンの第９交響曲とラフマニノフのピアノ協奏曲を演奏した。私は世の中にこんなにすばらしい音楽があるとは知らなかった。コンサートが終わったとき、私は音楽家になることを決意した。」

翌1922年、18才まで芸術音楽を知らず、楽譜も読めなかった青年は、新設されたグネーシン音楽専門学校のチェロ科に入学する。民族楽器を巧みにあやつり、また100余曲の民謡旋律を口ずさむことができたことも幸いした。1925年には学長M.F. グネーシンの勧めで、彼はチェロ科からグネーシンの作曲クラスに転入する。彼に当時のハチャトゥリャンのことを、グネーシンはこう語っている―――「彼はみがかれざる宝石である」と。

1929年、26才のハチャトゥリャンはモスクワ音楽院に入学、カバレフスキーやシェバーリンの師でもあった大家、ニコライ・ミャスコフスキーに師事、アカデミズムにますますみがきをかける。

1932年には初めてプロコフィエフと出会うが、プロコフィエフはハチャトゥリャンの〈クラリネットとヴァイオリンとピアノのためのトリオ〉に助言を与え、またその楽譜の出版にも力を貸している。

母校モスクワ音楽院卒業時に〈交響曲第１番〉を作曲したハチャトゥリャンは、ピアノ協奏曲、そしてヴァイオリン協奏曲と、傑作を次々に発表、世界的な注目を集める。そして後の傑作《ガイーヌ》とともにこの《スパルタクス》もまた今日もなお世界中で親しまれているバレエ音楽のひとつとなったのである。

ハチャトゥリャンは、その生涯にバレエ音楽を３曲発表している(現存するものは２曲)。

第１作目は1939年の《幸福》であるが、しかし作曲者は後にこれを《ガイーヌ》に転用し、1942年に初演。このハチャトゥリャンの代名詞とも言えるバレエはスターリン賞を受賞した。そして第３作目となるのが1959年、レーニン賞受賞の《スパルタクス》である。周知のとおり、《スパルタクス》は、紀元前73年から71年にかけて、古代ローマに起こった奴隷反乱の指導者で、その自由と解放を求めた闘士スパルタクスの不屈の精神は、ヴォルコフの台本、そしてハチャト

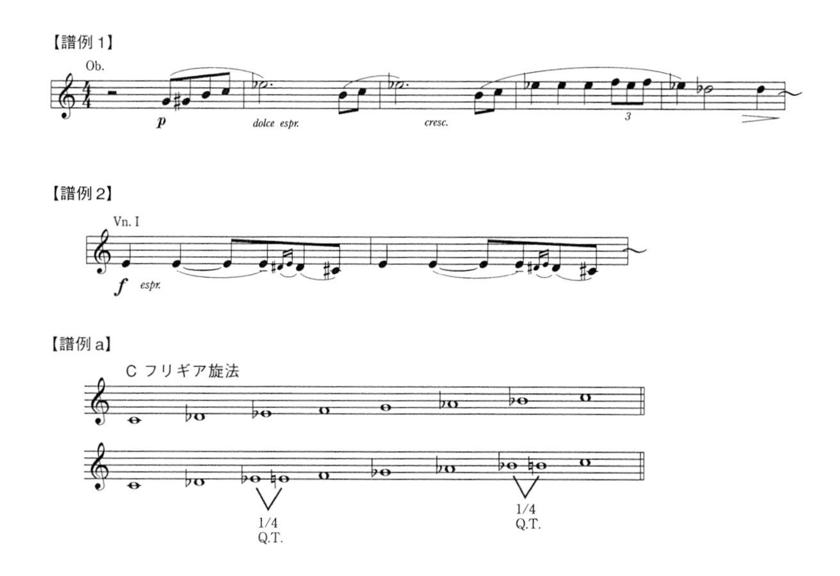

ゥリャンの音楽によって再び蘇ったのである。オリジナルは全4幕9場から成り、1950年から54年にかけてスターラヤ・ルーザの作曲家の創造の家で作曲された。初演は1956年12月27日、レニングラードのキーロフ劇場で行われたが、その時の振付はヤコブソンであった（後1957～58年改訂）。ちなみにスパルタクスとこのバレエ音楽の作曲の契機について、作曲者自身次の様に述べている――。

「スパルタクスの勇敢な英雄的な人物像はずっと以前から私の心を惹きつけ、バレエの作曲を促していた・・・・古代ローマにおけるスパルタクスと奴隷蜂起の主題は、今日のわれわれの社会でもきわめて大きな衝撃的な意義をもつように思われる」アラム・ハチャトゥリャン（ユゼフォーヴィチ 著『ハチャトゥリャン』より――小林久枝訳〔音楽之友社〕） また、総譜中に音楽の演劇性が明確に感じとれることを目指し、そのためにチャイコフスキー、グラズノフ等のロシア・バレエ音楽のクラシックを手本にしたことも自身告白している。また、振付に関しては、初演時のヤコブソンのものに続いて、モイセーエフ、チャンガ、そして現在でも最もポピュラーな演出として知られるグリゴローヴィチの手によるもの等があることを付記しておこう。なおここでは組曲版に基づいて解説をすすめていくが、作品にはやはり作曲者の故国、アルメニア音楽の要素が色濃く、この伝統音楽を抜きしてハチャトゥリャンの芸術を語ることはやはり不可能であることが再認識されるだろう――。

なおオーケストラ編成は次のとおり。

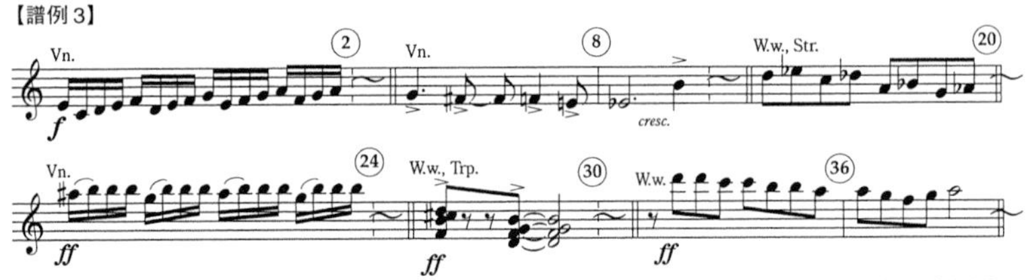

※丸囲みの数字は、小節番号

編成

フルート 2、ピッコロ（フルート3番持ち替え）、オーボエ 2、イングリッシュ・ホルン（F管）、クラリネット（B♭管） 2、バス・クラリネット(B♭管)（クラリネット3番持ち替え）、ファゴット 2

ホルン（F管） 4、トランペット（B♭管） 4、トロンボーン 3、テューバ

ティンパニ、トライアングル、タンブリン、ウッドブロック、小太鼓、シンバル、大太鼓、タムタム

シロフォン（木琴）、ハープ、ピアノ

ヴァイオリン I、ヴァイオリン II、ヴィオラ、チェロ、コントラバス

第2組曲

1．スパルタクスとフリーギアのアダージョ

Adagio 4/4

11小節間の序奏部を経て次の12小節目3拍目からオーボエが弦楽とハープの分散和音上に変イ長調の叙情的なテーマを奏する〔譜例1〕。[2]から曲はpoco più mosso へと変わり、やや速度を増すが、テンポは常にゆれ動く。[3]からこのテーマは変ニ長調でくり返され[4]のSostenutoで速度をおとすと[5]からa tempoへと変化、嬰ト音上にヴァイオリンが新たな主題を奏する〔譜例2〕。このテーマはひきのばされて[8]に達すると、テンポは突然più mossoへと変わり、フリギア旋法のテーマがトランペットの相づちをともなってあらわれる。ここでは主に第3、第7音の半音変化を常にともなっているのが特色である〔a〕。このフリギア旋法によるテーマはさまざまなゼクエンツによって高揚発展し、[12]でTempo I、***ff***に達すると、オーケストラはトゥッティにより、冒頭での変イ長調のテーマ〔譜例1〕を今度は変ニ長調で再現する。これは[13]から再びニ長調であらわれ[14]のコーダへと流れ込んでいく。ここのコーダの要素もまた冒頭〔譜例1〕のテーマからとられている。曲全体の構成は序奏―A―B―C―A―coda。

2．商人の入場～ローマ人遊女の踊り～全体の踊り

曲全体は大きくAllegro vivace 4/4 のA部分[1]～Moderato のB部分[6]～Allegro vivace のC部分[11]～ の3つに分けることが

できる。

まずA部分はほぼ一貫するオスティナート上にくり広げられるさまざまなリズムモティーフ〔譜例3〕によるテーマの対比が特長的な自由な構成とみることができる。これらはあらわれては消え、また突然姿をあらわす。A部分は6の直前で「イ」音に終止、次の6 ModeratoでB部分に入る。ここでは4分音符がきざむリズムによって7からまずフルート、クラリネット、トランペットそしてオーボエが対話をかわすが、主旋律はクラリネットが吹く。8のa tempoからはこのテーマが変奏されて反復、9のフェルマータを経てクラリネットのカデンツァの後、今度は10からヴァイオリンが新たなテーマを奏する。それをファゴットが模倣しながら11の手前でB部分を終える。11からのC部分は13の手前までが序奏、13からDエオリア旋法によるシンコペーションを特長としたテーマがまず管と弦により奏される。14からはA部分36小節からのリズムモティーフによるテーマが再びあらわれ、これは変拍子によってフレーズにより変化が与えられる。16からはDエオリア旋法によるテーマの再現。あとは打楽器のリズムにのってたたみこむようにテンポを速めて終止し、アタッカによってすぐさま次の曲へと入る。

3．スパルタクスの入場～指揮官の反目～ハーモディアスの背信

曲全体は1 Lento 4/4 ～5手前までがA
5 Andante 4/4 ～13手前までがB
13 Andante ～ おわりまでがC
の3つの部分から成る。

まず、A部分はLentoによるゆるやかな部分と、快速な部分とが変拍子及び、アクセントをもったシンコペーションのリズムとで対比させられているのが特長的である。11小節目 Allegro vivace で、まずスパルタクス入場のファンファーレ〔譜例4〕がトラン

ペットによって奏されるが、これは再度[3]の2小節目から移調、変形されて吹かれる。B [5] からテンポは Andante に変わり、ヴァイオリンがGフリギア旋法によるテーマを奏する〔b〕。[6] からテンポは♩= 152へと変わり、減5度から成るペンタトニックによるオスティナート・バス〔c〕上に[13] 手前まで華麗なオーケストレーションがくり広げられる。ここでもまた「ハ」「嬰ハ」及び「ニ」「嬰ニ」音が常時ぶつかり合っていることに気がつく。[12] からテンポはゆるやかになり[13] のAndante からC。ここでは主に管と弦楽器によるテーマの対話が続く。おしまいはニ音上に弦楽とティンパニ、そしてフルートが長三和音を奏でながら曲は静かに終止する。

まず、完全5度、完全4度を積み重ねた空虚な響きの冒頭2小節間につづいて、木管と弦楽器は8分音符による分散クロマティック和音で応ずる。この7小節間が序奏部であるが [2] から奏されるトランペットを中心とするテーマ〔譜例5〕はここ序奏部のリズムモティーフからとられている。拍子をめまぐるしく変化させながら、ペンタトニックに基づくオスティナート・バス〔d〕上に[3] の直前から再びトランペットによって副次テーマが吹かれる〔譜例6〕。副次テーマはひきのばされて [7] に至ると同時に [2] のテーマ〔譜例5〕が再現、尚コーダ部分はこの再現部に組み込まれていると見なすのが妥当だろう。

4. 略奪者の踊り

Allegro vivace　4/4

第２組曲は主に第３幕の音楽から取られている。

１．**スパルタクスとフリーギアのアダージョ**（第３幕･第７場、スパルタクスの野営地における愛のデュエット）

２．**商人の入場～ローマ人遊女の踊り～全体の踊り**（第３幕･第７場、戦士たちや民衆がおどけた踊りをするシーン）

３．**スパルタクスの入場～指揮官の反目～ハーモディアスの背信**（第３幕･第７場）

４．**略奪者の踊り**（出自不明）

Aram Khachaturian: "Spartacus" Second Suite from the Ballet

Commentary by Koichi Owa

Aram Ilych Khachaturian (1903-1978), along with Prokofiev, Shostakovich and Kabalevsky among others, was one of the composers representing the Soviet musical community in the 20th century. His most famous works include the ballets *Gayaneh* and *Spartacus*, *Masquerade* incidental to a theatrical play of the same title, and three symphonies, of which No. 2 *"The Bell Symphony"* is particularly well known. In the field of concertos, those for piano and violin seem to be most frequently performed. Now, let us see how he grew up into a great composer.

Khachaturian was an Armenian born in 1903 in Kozhor Village (Tbilisi City, Georgia). The area was a treasure-house of folk music from Armenia, Azerbaidzhan and Georgia, also a hot springs resort which had thrived since the days of the Russian Empire.

Aram's father was a bookbinder, and the musical environment surrounding him was nothing of a kind abound in Western academism, or the classical music of the 18th and 19th century Europe. The music Khachaturian encountered was folk songs and folk music of his homeland. One can well say that they remained the root of creation, or the core for the composer all his life. He spoke of his encounter with the "music" in this way.

"When I was a little boy, mother used to sing me Armenian and Azerbaidzhani folk songs very expressively. I let one of them, a song of a sad hunter, mellow in my mind for a long time, and it eventually became the basis of a theme in the second movement of my *Symphony No. 2*. In town, too, music surrounded me. I heard Georgian choruses and the plucking of Azerbaidzhani string instruments, and I would listen to roving folk poets and singers for hours. The musical passion of people around me as a little boy, and the forms, intonations and rhythms of their sounds have permeated my works at the subconscious level like 'mother's milk'." "When I was seven years old, I was instinctively attracted by and marveled at the spell of folk music, if only in a childlike way. I remember I sneaked into the attic, and tried to reproduce the ethnic rhythm I had overheard and been impressed with by striking whatever I found there, trying many variations and combinations. In this way, my first musical activities gave me too great a joy to express in words, but they drove my parents into despair..."

In the meantime, however, when the Khachaturians moved to another house, they were fortunate enough to buy an old piano from the former occupant of their house at a low price.

"I immediately began to play the melodies of folk songs and dances, trying to find the right keys for the sounds my ears remembered. Filled with an inexplicable sense of satisfaction, I endlessly repeated each melody with one finger or two, and learned it by rote..." This is what Japanese composer Nobuo Terahara directly heard from his teacher Khachaturian (quoted from Terahara's commentary entitled "Growing Up Surrounded by Folk Music" appended to a CD published by Victor Musical Industries Inc. in Japan).

In 1921, then 18 years old, Aram left for Moscow, together with his older brother Sulen. It was after the establishment of a Soviet regime in Georgia. At the brother's advice, he became an auditor in the preliminary course of the physics and mathematics department of the Moscow University Faculty of Biology. However, then occurred his impressive encounter with 'music' which decided the way of his later life.

"When I happened to pass by the Moscow Conservatory of Music together with my brother, I found a notice of a concert, and entered the concert hall. Inside the beautiful hall, there were portraits of great musicians hung on the wall. The orchestra played Beethoven's *Symphony No. 9* and *Piano Concerto* by Rachmaninov. I did not know such wonderful works of music had existed in the world. By the end of the concert, I had made up my mind to become a musician."

In the following year, 1922, the youth who had known neither artistic music nor how to read written music until the age of 18 entered the cello department of the newly opened Gnesin School of Music. His skills in playing folk instruments and memory of more than 100 folk melodies helped him find his way into the music school. In 1925, at the recommendation of rector M.F. Gnesin, Khachaturian transferred from the cello department to Gnesin's own composition class. Later, Gnesin commented on Khachaturian as he found him then, saying: "He was a gem in the rough."

In 1929, then 26 years old Khachaturian entered the Moscow Conservatory of Music, where he studied under Nikolay Myaskovsky, also the teacher of Kabalevsky and Sheberin, and further polished up his academism.

In 1932, Khachaturian met Prokofiev for the first time. Prokofiev gave advice on Khachaturian's *Trio for Clarinet, Violin and Piano*, and helped him make arrangements for publication of this work.

Composing *Symphony No. 1* at the time of graduating from the Moscow Conservatory, Khachaturian attracted worldwide note by successively turning out such masterpieces as the *Piano Concerto* and the *Violin Concerto*. And this *Spartacus*, along with the later masterpiece Gayaneh, retains a position among the best loved ballet music works in the world today.

Khachaturian published three ballets in his lifetime (two of which remain today).

The first was *Shchastye* (Happiness) in 1939, but the composer diverted substantial elements of the work to *Gayaneh*, which was premiered in 1942. This ballet, whose title is almost a synonym to the composer's name, won a Stalin Prize. The third was *Spartacus*, winning a Lenin Prize in 1959. As is well known, Spartacus was the leader of slave uprising in ancient Rome from 73 till 71 B.C. The indomitable spirit of fighter Spartacus struggling for freedom and liberation revived through the libretto by Nikolay Volkov and the music by Khachaturian. The original, consisting of four acts in nine scenes, was composed from 1950 to 1954 in the Composers House of Creativity in Old Rouza. The ballet was premiered on December 27, 1956 at the Kirov Theater in Leningrad with choreography by Leonid Yakobson (later revised from 1957 to 58). Incidentally, the composer said in his own words about Spartacus and what motivated him to compose the ballet music taking the theme from this ancient hero: "The courageous and heroic personality of Spartacus had long attracted my heart and urged me to compose a ballet having him as its hero... The theme of Spartacus and slaves' uprising in ancient Rome seems to have a great and shocking significance even to our society of today" (quoted from Victor Yuzefovich, *Aram Khachaturyan*, retranslated from the Japanese translation by Ms. Hisae Kobayashi). Khachaturian further confessed that he, with a view to making the drama of the music vividly sensible in the score, had taken models from the classics of Russian ballet music by Tchaikovsky and Glazunov among others. It may be worth mentioning here that choreographic versions of *Spartacus* include, Yakobson's for the premiere, those by Igor Moiseev, Changa, and Yury Nikolayevich Grigorovich, the last being most popular today. While the following commentary will basically refer to the suites derived from the ballet, it will remind the reader again of the significant presence of the elements of Armenian music, the music of the composer's homeland, in his works and of the impossibility to discuss Khachaturian's art without reference to this traditional music.

The instrumentation is as follows.

2 Flutes

Piccolo (played by the third flutist)

2 Oboes

English horn (F)

2 Clarinets (B flat)

Bass clarinet (B flat) (played by the third clarinetist)

2 Bassoons

4 Horns (F)

4 Trumpets (B flat)

3 Trombones

Tuba

Timpani

Triangle

Tambourine

Wood blocks [Legno]

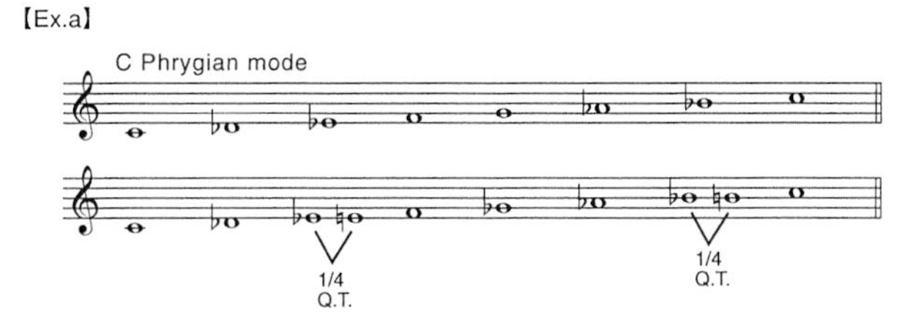

Cymbals [Piatti]
Bass drum [Cassa]
Tam-tam
Xylophone [Silofono]
Harp [Arpa]
Piano
Violins I
Violins II
Violas
Violoncellos
Double basses

Second Suite

1. Adagio of Spartacus and Phrygia

Adagio, 4/4

After an 11-bar introduction, from the third beat of the next 12th bar onward, the oboes play a lyric theme in A flat major over arpeggios by the strings and harp (Ex. 1). At [2], the tune changes to *poco più mosso*, a little faster, but the tempo constantly fluctuates. From [3] onward, this theme is repeated in D flat major and, after slowing down at *sostenuto* marked at [4], changes to a tempo, and the violins play a new theme over a G sharp note (Ex. 2). When this theme is stretched to reach [8], the tempo suddenly changes to *più mosso*, and a theme in Phrygian mode emerges with nodding by the trumpets. Characteristically, it always involves chromatic changes of mainly the third and seventh notes (Ex. a). This theme in Phrygian mode is developed to sublimity in various forms of *sequenz* and, when *Tempo I*,

【Ex.3】

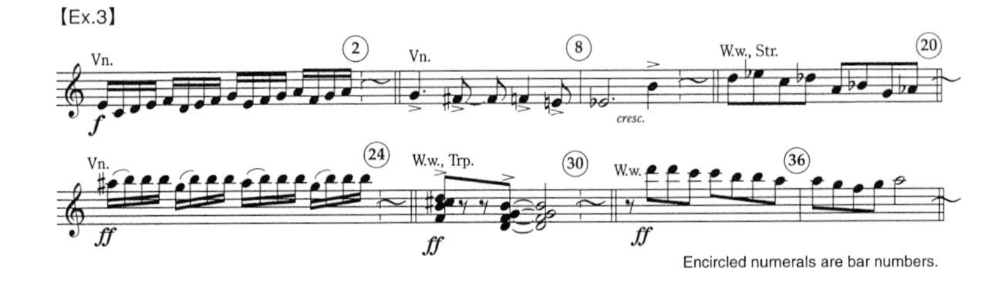

ff is reached at [12], the orchestra *tutti* recapitulates the theme, which was in A flat major at the beginning (Ex. 1), in D flat major this time. This theme again appears in D major [13] and flows into the coda at [14]. The element of this coda also is taken from the theme at the beginning (Ex. 1). The overall structure of the music is in an introduction-A-B-C-A-coda pattern.

2. Entrance of the Merchants, Dance of the Roman Courtesan, General Dance

The whole movement can be broadly divided into Part A of *Allegro vivace*, 4/4 (from [1] on), Part B of *Moderato* (from [6] on) and Part C of *Allegro vivace* (from [11] on).

First, Part A can be considered to have a free structure characterized by the contrasting of themes based on diverse rhythmic motifs (Ex. 3), developed over an almost uninterrupted continuation of *ostinato*. They appear and disappear, and suddenly emerge again. Part ends on an A note immediately before [6], and then Part B starts at next [6], *Moderato*. Here, first the flutes, clarinets, trumpets and oboes have dialogues with each other on a rhythm ticked in crotchets from [7] onward, and the main melody is played by the clarinets. From *a tempo* at [8] on, this theme is repeated in a varied way and, after a *cadenza* by the clarinets following *fermata* at [9], now the violins play a new theme from [10] onward. While this theme is imitated by the bassoons, Part B ends before [11]. Part C from [11] has an introduction until before [13], from where a theme characterized by syncopation in D Aeolian mode is played first by wind and string instruments. From [14] on, the theme on the rhythmic motifs from the 36th bar onward in Part A reemerges, and is varied from phrase to phrase in irregular time. From [16] on, the theme in D Aeolian mode is recapitulated. Then the movement ends at accelerated tempo as if to unfold itself riding on the rhythm of the percussions, and the next movement immediately begins *attacca*.

3. Entrance of Spartacus, The Quarrel, Treachery of Harmodius

The whole movement consists of Part A from [1] until before [5], *Lento*, 4/4, Part B

【Ex.4】

【Ex.b】

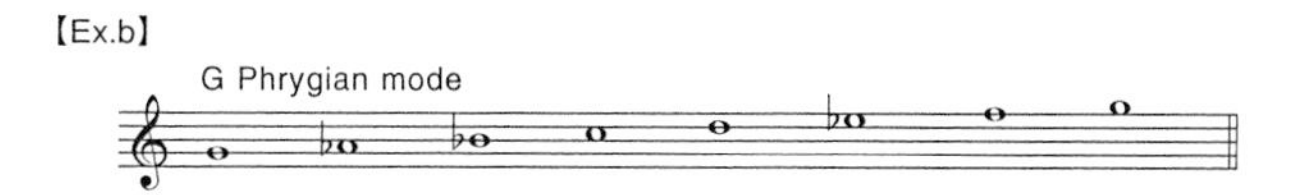

【Ex.c】

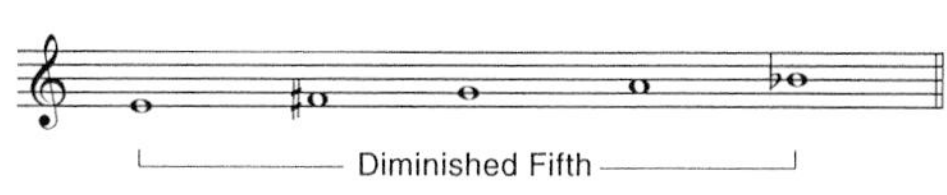

【Ex.5】

【Ex.d】

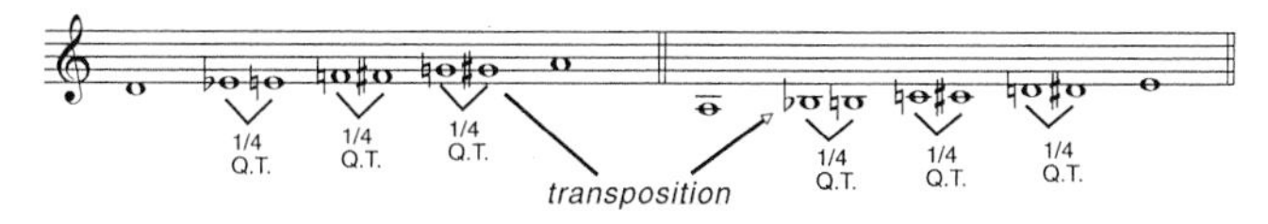

【Ex.6】

from [5] until before [13], *Andante*, 4/4 and Part C from [13] until the end, *Andante*.

First, Part A is characterized by a contrast between a slow *Lento* subpart and a fast one presented with irregular time and accentuated syncopated rhythm. At the 11th bar, *Allegro vivace*, first a fanfare announcing the entrance of Spartacus is blown by the trumpets (Ex. 4), and it is played again from the second bar after [3], this time in a transposed and transformed way. At [5] in Part B, the tempo changes to *Andante*, and the violins play a theme in G Phrygian mode (Ex. b). At [6], the tempo changes to ♩=152, and brilliant orchestration is developed on *ostinato* bass (Ex. c) by pentatonism of diminished fifth. It is noticed that here again there are constant clashes between C and C sharp and between D and D sharp notes. The tempo slows down at [13], and Part C begins at [13], *Andante*. The movement comes to a calm end as the strings, timpani and flutes play a major triad over a D note.

4. Dance of the Pirates

Allegro vivace, 4/4

Following the first two bars of hollow sounds in which a perfect fifth and a perfect fourth are stacked one over the other, the woodwinds and strings respond with chromatic arpeggios. Whereas these seven bars constitute the introduction, the theme played mainly by the trumpets (Ex. 5) from [7] onward is taken from the rhythmic motif of this introduction. While the time is being bewilderingly changed, a secondary theme is blown by the trumpets again from immediately before [3] onward over *ostinato* bass (Ex. d) based on pentatonism (Ex. 6). The secondary theme is stretched until [7] and at the same time the theme from [2] on (Ex. 5) is recapitulated. It will be appropriate to regard the coda part as being incorporated into this recapitulation.

Movements of the *Second Suite* mainly derive from music in the third act.

1. Adagio of Spartacus and Phrygia (Act 3, Scene 7: A duet of love at the field camp of Spartacus)
2. Entrance of the Merchants, Dance of the Roman Courtesan, General Dance (Act 3, Scene 7: Warriors and townsmen dance humorously.)
3. Entrance of Spartacus, The Quarrel, Treachery of Harmodius (Act 3, Scene 7)
4. Dance of the Pirates (Source unidentified)

Translated by Hiromichi Matsui

Spartacus

Second Suite

1. Adagio of Spartacus and Phrygia

Aram Khachaturian

Fl.
Cl.(Si♭)
Arpa
poco rit.
Ob.
I solo
div.

2 Poco più mosso (♩ = 72)
I
Ob.
dolce espress.
cresc.
Cl.(Si♭)
p
p
Arpa
unis.
pp
pp
pp
mp
espress.
poco ten.
a tempo
poco ten.
Fl.
Fl. a 2
f
Ob.
Cl.(Si♭)
Cl.
cresc.
cresc.
Arpa
mf
espress.

a tempo
poco rit.
a tempo
I solo
Fl.
Ob.
Cl.(Si♭)
Arpa
p espress.
Cor.(Fa)
Timp.
Cl. III muta in Cl.basso
cresc.
div.

3
mf
cresc.
f
mf
cresc.
f
mf
Arpa
Piano
mf
3
mf
cresc.
f
espress.
f
espress.
unis.
mf
pizz.
mf
pizz.
unis.
div.
mf
cresc.
mf

soli
f
Arpa
Piano
3
3

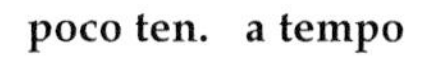
poco ten. a tempo

poco ten.
soli
poco ten. a tempo
poco ten.

a tempo
poco rit.
Cor.(Fa)
Timp.
Arpa
Piano
a tempo
poco ten.
a tempo
poco
a
Cor.(Fa)
Timp.
Arpa
Piano

poco
acceler.
cresc.
poco
acceler.

4 Sostenuto
poco string. rit.
f
p
mf
f
Arpa
Piano
4 Sostenuto
poco string. rit.
f ritard.
mf
arco

a tempo
5
Arpa
mp
poco a poco cresc.
f espress. poco a poco cresc.
p
mp
pizz.
p
molto rit.
I solo
a tempo
Cl.(Si♭)
Arpa
sul G ten.
string.
I
Cl.(Si♭)
Arpa
poco rit.

I solo
Ob.
mf dolce
I
Cl.(Si♭)
6
Cor.(Fa)
p
p
Arpa
f espress.
molto rit.
a tempo
I solo
Fl.
I solo
f
Ob.
f
Cor.(Fa)
p
Arpa
ten.

string.
Fl.
Ob.
or.(Fa)
Arpa
I
3
p
Fl.
Ob.
Fag.
I solo
p dolce
mf
7
I.II
p
div.
arco
pizz.
f espress.

molto rit.
a tempo
Cor.(Fa)
Arpa
mf
ten.
string.
Cor.(Fa)
mf
mf
Arpa
f
ff
mf
f
ff

8 Più mosso (♩ = 100-104)
Cor.(Fa)
-be(Si♭)
Tr-ni.
a 2
III mf cantabile
mf cantabile
1
mp
Timp.
mf
mf cantab.
arco
mf
poco a poco cresc. e acceler.
9 soli
f soli
f
or.(Fa)
-be(Si♭)
I
f
p
Timp.
Arpa p
Piano p
8
mf espress.
mf espress.
mf espress.
mp
mp

Fl.
Ob.
C. ingl.
Cl.
Cl. b.
Fg.
I
mf
Timp.
P-tti
p cresc.
Arpa
Piano
8
pizz.
f
arco
p cresc.
pizz.
f
arco
p cresc.
pizz.
f
arco
p cresc.

10
(♩= 160)
a 2
f
II
p
cresc.
Timp.
T-ro
mf
P-tti
Arpa
P-no
8
unis.

accelerando
mf
mf
accelerando
f
f
f
f
f

11
molto ritard.
a 2
mp cresc.
f
T-tam
p cresc.
11
molto ritard.
cresc.
mp

12 Tempo I
a 2
ff
f
I
mf cantab.
P-tti
Cassa
T-tam
mf
Arpa
P-no
12 Tempo I
molto espress.
ff vibrato

a 2
I

poco rit.
a tempo
rit.
Picc. muta in Fl. III
poco rit.
a tempo
rit.

a tempo
III
I
I
13
a tempo
13
p dolce
espress.
pizz.
pizz.

Cl.
Cor.
Arpa
Cl.
Cor.
Arpa

poco rit.
Cl.
Cor.
Arpa
a tempo
molto rit.
Cl.
Cor.
Arpa
solo
p espress.
arco

14 Lento
Fl.
p
div.
p

P-no
mf
div.
unis.
p
cresc. molto
ff
pp
pizz.
arco
p
mf

2. Entrance of the Merchants, Dance of the Roman Courtesan, General Dance

Cl.
Fag.
Cor.
P-tti
Arpa
mf
f
detaché
Ob.
C.ingl.
Cl.
Fag.
Cor.
Timp.
Arpa
cresc.

a 2
III
T-no
T-ro
P-tti
Cassa
Arpa
secco
secco
secco
secco
secco

a 2
III
colla bacch. di timp.

2 L'istesso tempo
a 2
T-ro
P-tti
Cassa
Tam-tam
Sil.
2 L'istesso tempo
détaché
pizz.

a 2
ff
III
ff
ff
ff
ff
a 2
ff
basso marcato
T-ro
P-tti
Cassa
basso marcato

3
ff
ff
ff
f
f
T-ro
P-tti
Cassa
Sil.
f
3
ff marc.
ff marc.
ff marc.
ff marc.

T-ro
P-tti
Cassa
Sil.
P-no
ff marc.
arco
pizz.

a 2
ff
f
T-ro
P-tti
Cassa
P-no
arco

4
5
ff
I
II
f

a2
f
a2
a2
f
a2
f
I
II
T-ro
P-tti
Cassa
P-no
f
f
f
f marc.
f marc.

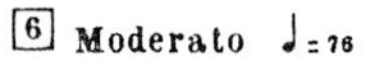
6 Moderato 𝅗𝅥 = 76

ff
T-no
mf
Arpa
f
poco a poco dim.
6 Moderato 𝅗𝅥 = 76
f poco a poco dim.

7
Fl.
Cl.
Tr-ba
T-no
Arpa
I solo
I con sord.
Ob.

poco ritardando
8
a tempo
I
mf
I solo
p dolce
3
ff
con sord.
p
I
colla bacch. di timp.
P-tti
T-tam
f
Do♯, Re♭, Fa♭, La♯, Si♭
mp
pizz.

Fl.
I
9
Cl. I solo
ad libitum
Fag.
Cor.
f
I
p
Tr-be
T-tam
p cresc. mf
Arpa
Cl. I
Cl. I
poco rit.

10
Fag.
I solo
mf espress.
Cor. f
f
Tr-ba I con sord.
mf
Arpa f
V-no solo
mp espress.
div.
pp
non div.
mf
pp
mf
pp
pizz.
arco
p
pp
pizz.
p
pp
Fag.
unis.

poco acceler.
Fag. I
V-no solo
3
3

a tempo
rit.
Lento
Arpa
p
pp
3

V-no solo
div a 3
3
pp

Allegro vivace ♩= 168
11
p cresc.
II-III sole
con sord.
soli
T-ro
P-tti
Cassa
P-no
pizz.
unis.
f

12

f

f

f

f

mf

I solo

con sord. f

mf

T-ro

P-tti

mf

Cassa

mf

ff Arpa

ff P-no

12

f

f

f

T-ro
P-tti
Cassa
Arpa
P-no

13
a2
sola
f
p
T-ro
mf
13

14
a2
ff
senza sord. I. II sole
f secco
III con sord.
Tr-lo
T-no
T-ro
Legno
p
cresc.
14
p

a2
ff
III (con sord.)
Tr-lo
T-no
T-ro
Legno
mf
f

I.II sole
(senza sord.)
f secco
T-no
f
Legno
p
cresc.
p
p
f
f
mf
f

15
a2
ff
soli
f
a2 sole
T-ro
P.tti
Cassa
p
cresc.
ff détaché
arco

ff
a2
soli
f
T-ro
P-tti
Cassa
p cresc.

a 2
f
T-ro
P-tti
Cassa

16
sola
T-ro
P-tti
Cassa
16

poco a poco cresc. ed molto acceler.
sub. p
T-ro
P-tti
poco a poco cresc. ed molto acceler.
attacca

3. Entrance of Spartacus, The Quarrel, Treachery of Harmodius

2 Lento ♩= 72
Cor.
poco cresc. e marc.
f
T-ro
ff espress.
arco
p
Allegro vivace ♩= 152
Cl.
Fag.
Tr-ba
I sola
Arpa
P-no
simile
pizz.

marcato
secco
p cresc.
T-ro
p
cresc.

Cor. I-IV a 2
Tr-be
Tr-ni
T-ro
Arpa
P-no
3
♩=152
I sola
marc.
sim.
Tr-ba I
cresc.

4
p cresc.
f
T-ro
P-tti
colla bacch. di timp.
f secco
ff
pizz.
arco
p

5 Andante ♩ = 80
Fag.
Cor.
Tr-ni
I.II
T-ro
Arpa
P-no
sul G
molto espress.
div.
arco
pizz.
T-tam
cresc.
unis. arco

poco rit.
6 ♩ = 152
Fag.
Cor.
I.II
T-ro
Arpa
mf marc.
mp
Fag.
Cor. I.II
T-ro
P-no
f marc.
f marc.

Fag.
P-no
Cl.
Fag.
f
a 2
f
Cor.
a 2
f
Timp.
p cresc.
P-no
p
f
p
f
p

7
a2
f
con sord.
f
con sord.
f
I.II soli
f
III sole
f
P-tti
f colla bacch. di timp.
f
P-no
7
p secco
p secco

8
I
f
3
p
Arpa
P-no
8

p
cresc. molto
f
p
cresc. molto
f
T-no
T-ro
p
cresc.
f
Arpa
ff
P-no
pizz.
f marc.
ff
pizz.
ff
pizz.
ff
pizz.
p
pizz.
p

9
III
mf
f
I
p cantabile poco a
cresc. molto
f
mf cantabile poco a
III solo
T-no
T-ro
p cresc.
ff
arco
p poco a
pp
poco a

a 2
f
f
f
I
poco cresc.
poco cresc.
III
poco cresc.
f
poco cresc. mp
mp poco cresc.
poco cresc.
poco cresc.
poco cresc.

P-no

10
I
f
Tuba
mf
T-no
T-ro
P-tti
p cresc.
f
Arpa
P-no
p
8
10
pizz.
arco
mf
III

sola
sole
P-tti
cresc.
arco
mf
f

11
soli
soli
T-no
P-tti
colla bacch. di timp.
P-no
11
sub. p poco a poco
sub. p poco a poco

sul p molto cresc.
a 2
mf cresc.
a 2
mf cresc.
sf
p cresc.
T-no
P-tti
T-tam
f
mf
p
8
cresc.

a2
III
I
II.III a2
P-tti
Cassa
T-tam
Arpa
do#, reb, fab, la#, sib
P-no
cresc.
cresc.
cresc.
cresc.
cresc.

12
P-tti
Cassa
Arpa
12
pizz.
mf pizz.
pizz.
soli
f
pizz.

13 **Andante** ♩ = 88

Fl. I
p
Arpa
div.
Fl.
14
Arpa
div.

Fl.
Cl.
Fag.
I solo
Cor.
T-tam
Arpa
div.
p dolce
unis.
pizz.
15 Poco meno mosso (Andante) ♩=78
poco rit.
(I solo)
Cor. a 2
III
pp
arco

Fl. I solo
16
Cl.
I solo
p
I +
Cor.
Arpa
3
molto rit.
Fl. I
p
Cl.
Cor.
Timp.
p
Arpa
tutti
pizz.
p
pizz.
p

4. Dance of the Pirates

Tr-lo
T-no
T-ro
ff
f
mf cresc.
arco
pizz.
arco

2
a 2
ff
I
f
II
pizz.

a 2
a 2
a 2
I
II
I
III
T-lo
T-no
T-ro

a 2
a 2
a 2
mf marc.
mf marc.
II
f
III
f
II.III sole
f
mf
mf
Tr-lo
T-no
T-ro
mf
P-tti
mf
Cassa
mf

a 2
ff
ff
ff
ff
I sola
f
II sola
f
T-ro
P-tti
Cassa
f
mf
mf
pizz.
pizz.

3
a2
ff
I
II
T-ro
P-tti
Cassa
3

4
ff
ff
ff
ff
ff
ff
ff
ff
4

a 2
ff
II
soli
f

5
ff
ff
ff
ff
I
f
II
f
5
ff
ff
ff

6
7
p
cresc.
soli
f
P-no
ff
8
arco

a 2
ff
I
II
f
Tr-lo
T-no
T ro
pizz.

a 2
a 2
a 2
a 2
8
soli
soli
II
I
III
soli
soli
8

a2
a2
a2
a2
a2
T-no
T-ro
arco

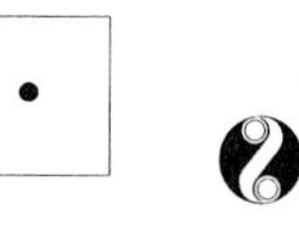

2308084

ハチャトゥリャン
《スパルタクス》第２組曲
解説——大輪公壱
第１版第１刷発行——2009年11月15日
第１版第７刷発行——2023年 8月25日
発行——株式会社全音楽譜出版社
——東京都新宿区上落合２丁目13番３号 〒161-0034
——TEL 営業部 03・3227-6270
—— 出版部 03・3227-6280
——URL http://www.zen-on.co.jp/
——ISBN978-4-11-892561-5

ZEN-ON MINIATURE SCORES

スコア・リーディング "SCORE-READING" /rev. MOROI, Saburo
諸井三郎 編 (890001)

芥川也寸志 AKUTAGAWA, Yasushi
交響曲第1番* (893600)
交響三章* (893603)
交響管弦楽のための音楽* (893601)
チェロとオーケストラのためのコンチェルトオスティナート* (893602)
オルガンとオーケストラのための「響」* (893604)

アルチュニアン ARUTIUNIAN, Alexander
トランペット協奏曲*◆ (892701)

バッハ BACH, Johann Sebastian
管弦楽組曲 第1－4番 (890251)
ブランデンブルク協奏曲 全曲〔第1-6番〕* (897401) NEW

バルトーク BARTÓK, Béla
管弦楽のための協奏曲* (892531)
《中国の不思議な役人》組曲* (892530)

ベートーヴェン BEETHOVEN, Ludwig van
交響曲第1番ハ長調 作品21* (897001) NEW
交響曲第2番ニ長調 作品36* (897002) NEW
交響曲第3番変ホ長調 作品55「英雄」* (897003) NEW
交響曲第4番変ロ長調 作品60* (897004) NEW
交響曲第5番ハ短調 作品67* (897005) NEW
交響曲第6番ヘ長調 作品68「田園」* (897006) NEW
交響曲第7番イ長調 作品92* (897007) NEW
交響曲第8番ヘ長調 作品93* (897008) NEW
交響曲第9番ニ短調 作品125「合唱」* (897009) NEW
コリオラン序曲 作品62* (897021) NEW
エグモント序曲 作品84* (897024) NEW
《フィデリオ》序曲 作品72* (897023) NEW
レオノーレ序曲 第3番 作品72a* (897022) NEW
ピアノ協奏曲第1番ハ長調 作品15 (890541)
ピアノ協奏曲第2番変ロ長調 作品19 (890542)
ピアノ協奏曲第3番ハ短調 作品37* (897013) NEW
ピアノ協奏曲第4番ト長調 作品58* (897014) NEW
ピアノ協奏曲第5番変ホ長調 作品73「皇帝」* (897015) NEW
ヴァイオリン協奏曲ニ長調 作品61* (897016) NEW
弦楽四重奏曲集〔合本〕： 全巻 NEW
第1巻 (第1, 2, 3番 作品18 - 1, 2, 3) (897025)
第2巻 (第4, 5, 6番 作品18 - 4, 5, 6) (897026)
第3巻 (第7, 8, 9番 作品59 - 1, 2, 3〔ラズモフスキー〕) (897027)
第4巻 (第10番 作品74；第11番 作品95；第12番 作品127) (897028)
第5巻 (第13番 作品130；第14番 作品131；第15番 作品132) (897029)
第6巻 (第16番 作品135；大フーガ 作品133) (897030)

ベルリオーズ BERLIOZ, Hector
幻想交響曲 作品14* (897171) NEW

ビゼー BIZET, Georges
《アルルの女》組曲第1番・第2番〔全8曲〕* (897181)
《カルメン》組曲第1番・第2番〔全12曲〕* (890852)

ビゼー/シチェドリン BIZET / SHCHEDRIN
カルメン組曲*◆ (892511)

ボロディン BORODIN, Alexandre
交響曲第2番ロ短調*◆ (897202) NEW
中央アジアの草原にて* (897203) NEW
《イーゴリ公》- ポロヴェツ人の踊りと合唱*◆ (897201) NEW
《イーゴリ公》- 序曲／ポロヴェツ人の行進*◆ (897204) NEW

ブラームス BRAHMS, Johannes
交響曲第1番ハ短調 作品68* (897041) NEW
交響曲第2番ニ長調 作品73* (897042) NEW
交響曲第3番ヘ長調 作品90* (897043) NEW
交響曲第4番ホ短調 作品98* (897044) NEW
大学祝典序曲 作品80* (891121) NEW
悲劇的序曲 作品81* (891120) NEW
ピアノ協奏曲第1番ニ短調 作品15 (897051) NEW
ピアノ協奏曲第2番変ロ長調 作品83* (897052) NEW
ヴァイオリン協奏曲ニ長調 作品77 (891145)

ブラームス/シェーンベルク BRAHMS, J. - SCHOENBERG, A.
ピアノ四重奏曲第1番ト短調 作品25〔管弦楽編曲版〕* (891111)

シャブリエ CHABRIER, Emmanuel
オーケストラのための「ラメント」* (893506)

團 伊玖磨 DAN, Ikuma
古雅幻想曲* (893610)
4本のバスーンのためのソナタ* (893611)

ドビュッシー DEBUSSY, Claude
〈海〉― 3つの交響的素描* (897282) NEW
牧神の午後への前奏曲* (897281) NEW

ドリーブ DELIBES, Léo
バレエ組曲《コッペリア》〔抜粋：15曲〕* (892081) NEW
組曲《コッペリア》* (892082) NEW

デュカス DUKAS, Paul
交響詩「魔法使いの弟子」* (892060)

ドヴォルジャーク DVOŘÁK, Antonín
交響曲第7番ニ短調 作品70* (897081) NEW
交響曲第8番ト長調 作品88* (897082) NEW
交響曲第9番ホ短調 作品95「新世界から」* (897083) NEW
序曲「謝肉祭」作品92* (891421) NEW
スラヴ舞曲 第1集 (作品46 全曲) (891451)
チェロ協奏曲ロ短調 作品104* (897084) NEW

エルガー ELGAR, Edward
行進曲「威風堂々」第1番・第4番 作品39* (891455)

ファリャ FALLA, Manuel de
バレエ音楽《三角帽子》全曲* (892121) NEW
《はかなき人生》間奏曲とスペイン舞曲* (892122) NEW

フォーレ FAURÉ, Gabriel
シシリエンヌ 作品80-3 (ピアノ・リダクション付) (893501)

フランク FRANCK, César
交響曲ニ短調* (897191) NEW

深井史郎 FUKAI, Shiro
パロディ的な四楽章 (1936)〔ファクシミリ版〕* (893612)

グリエール GLIÈR, Reingol'd
バレエ組曲《赤いけし》作品70a* (892702)
バレエ組曲《青銅の騎士》作品89a* (892703)

グリンカ GLINKA, Mikhail
オペラ《ルスランとリュドミラ》序曲* (892641)

グリーク GRIEG, Eduard
《ペール・ギュント》組曲第1番・第2番〔全8曲〕* (891042) NEW
ピアノ協奏曲イ短調 作品16* (897271) NEW

ハイドン HAYDN, Josef
交響曲第94番ト長調「驚愕」 (890301)
交響曲第100番ト長調「軍隊」 (890302)
弦楽四重奏曲ハ長調 作品76-3「皇帝」 (890371)

ホルスト HOLST, Gustav
組曲「惑星」* (891471)

オネゲル HONEGGER, Arthur
交響曲第3番「典礼風交響曲」* (893543)
パシフィック231* (893541)
夏の牧歌* (893542)

カバレフスキー KABALEVSKY, Dmitri
「道化師」組曲 作品26*◆ (892501)

金子仁美 KANEKO, Hitomi
「連歌 II」― Fl, Cl, 打楽器, Pf, Vn, Vc. のための―* (893640)

ハチャトゥリャン KHACHATURIAN, Aram
交響曲第1番ホ短調*◆ (892569)
交響曲第2番*◆ (892558)
交響曲第3番「交響詩曲」*◆ (892559)
《ガイーヌ》- 第1組曲*◆ (892552)
《ガイーヌ》- 第2組曲*◆ (892553)
《ガイーヌ》- 第3組曲*◆ (892554)
《スパルタクス》- 第1組曲*◆ (892560)
《スパルタクス》- 第2組曲*◆ (892561)
《スパルタクス》- 第3組曲*◆ (892562)
《スパルタクス》による交響的絵画 (第4場・第5場)*◆ (892570)
《スパルタクス》による交響的絵画 (第9場)*◆ (892571)
《仮面舞踏会》組曲*◆ (892551)
《ヴァレンシアの未亡人 (寡婦)》組曲*◆ (892556)
劇音楽《リア王》*◆ (892566)
劇音楽《マクベス》*◆ (892567)
アルメニア・ドラマ・スタジオ作品集*◆ (892568)
チェロ協奏曲ホ短調*◆ (892573)
ピアノ協奏曲*◆ (892557)
ヴァイオリン協奏曲ニ短調*◆ (892555)
チェロとオーケストラのためのコンチェルト・ラプソディ*◆ (892563)
ピアノとオーケストラのためのコンチェルト・ラプソディ*◆ (892564)
ヴァイオリンとオーケストラのためのコンチェルト・ラプソディ*◆ (892565)

コダーイ KODÁLY, Zoltán
組曲《ハーリ・ヤーノシュ》* (890971)

コルンゴルト KORNGOLD, Erich Wolfgang
ヴァイオリン協奏曲ニ長調 作品35* (892581)

リスト LISZT, Franz
交響詩「レ・プレリュード」* (897261)
ハンガリー狂詩曲第2番 (ミュラー=ベルクハウス編)* (890952)

マーラー MAHLER, Gustav
交響曲第2番ハ短調「復活」 (891702)
交響曲第3番ニ短調 (891703)
交響曲第5番嬰ハ短調 (891705)
交響曲第10番 ― アダージョ* (891706)

マスネ MASSENET, Jules
組曲《絵のような風景》(管弦楽のための組曲第4番)* (893511) NEW

（＊印は A5 判または B5 変型判の読みやすい中型サイズです）（◆印は解説の英語訳つきです）

松村禎三　MATSUMURA, Teizo
- 弦楽のための「プネウマ」（松村禎三作品目録付）(893620)

メンデルスゾーン　MENDELSSOHN-Bartholdy, Felix
- 交響曲第 3 番イ短調 作品 56「スコットランド」* (897241) NEW
- 交響曲第 4 番イ長調 作品 90「イタリア」* (897242) NEW
- 交響曲第 5 番ニ短調 作品 105「宗教改革」* (891305) NEW
- ヴァイオリン協奏曲ホ短調 作品 64* (897243) NEW

モーツァルト　MOZART, Wolfgang Amadeus
- 交響曲第 35 番ニ長調 KV385「ハフナー」(890401)
- 交響曲第 36 番ハ長調 KV425「リンツ」(890402)
- 交響曲第 38 番ニ長調 KV504「プラハ」(890403)
- 交響曲第 39 番変ホ長調 KV543 (890404)
- 交響曲第 40 番ト短調 KV550* (890405) NEW
- 交響曲第 41 番ハ長調 KV551「ジュピター」* (897302) NEW
- ピアノ協奏曲 (第 20 番) ニ短調 KV466 (890442)
- ピアノ協奏曲 (第 23 番) イ長調 KV488 (890443)
- ピアノ協奏曲 (第 26 番) ニ長調 KV537「戴冠式」(890441)
- アイネ・クライネ・ナハトムジーク KV525* (890411) NEW
- クラリネット協奏曲イ長調 KV622 (890447)

ムソルグスキー　MUSSORGSKY, Modest
- 〈はげ山の一夜〉〔リムスキー＝コルサコフ編曲版〕* (897431) NEW
- 《ホヴァンシチナ》前奏曲〔2つの編曲版〕*◆ (892252)

ムソルグスキー／ラヴェル　MUSSORGSKY / RAVEL
- 組曲「展覧会の絵」* (892253)

西村 朗　NISHIMURA, Akira
- フルートと管楽と打楽器のための協奏曲* (893630)
- 流れ ～闇の訪れたあとに *A Stream - After Dark** (893631)

尾高尚忠　OTAKA, Hisatada
- 第一交響曲〔第 1, 2 楽章／ファクシミリ版〕*◆ (893613)
- フルート小協奏曲 作品 30a*◆ (893614)

プーランク　POULENC, Francis
- シンフォニエッタ* (893522) NEW
- ピアノ協奏曲* (893521)

プロコフィエフ　PROKOFIEV, Sergei
- 古典交響曲 (交響曲第 1 番) ニ長調 作品 25*◆ (892668)
- 交響曲第 5 番変ロ長調 作品 100* (892665)
- 交響曲第 6 番変ホ短調 作品 111* (892666)
- 交響曲第 7 番嬰ハ短調 作品 131*◆ (892667) a
- 「スキタイ組曲」作品 20*◆ (892678) NEW
- 組曲《3つのオレンジへの恋》作品 33-bis*◆ (892679) NEW
- 組曲《キージェ中尉》作品 60*◆ (892680) NEW
- 《シンデレラ》組曲第 1 番 作品 107* (892671)
- 《シンデレラ》組曲第 2 番 作品 108* (892672)
- 《シンデレラ》組曲第 3 番 作品 109* (892673)
- 「ピーターと狼」作品 67*[日本語ナレーション] (892670)
- 《ロメオとジュリエット》組曲第 1 番 作品 64-bis*◆ (892661)
- 《ロメオとジュリエット》組曲第 2 番 作品 64-ter*◆ (892662)
- 《ロメオとジュリエット》組曲第 3 番 作品 101*◆ (892663)
- オーケストラのための「ワルツ組曲」作品 110*◆ (892677)
- 交響組曲「1941 年」作品 90*◆ (892676)
- 「冬のかがり火」作品 122*◆ (892664)
- ピアノ協奏曲第 4 番 作品 53 (左手のための)*◆ (892674)
- チェロのためのコンチェルティーノ 作品 132*◆ (892675)
- 《アレクサンドル・ネフスキー》作品 78*◆ (892669)

ラフマニノフ　RACHMANINOFF, Sergei
- ピアノ協奏曲第 2 番ハ短調 作品 18* (892461)
- ピアノ協奏曲第 3 番ニ短調 作品 30* (892463)
- パガニーニの主題による狂詩曲 作品 43* (892462)

ラヴェル　RAVEL, Maurice
- ボレロ* (892472)
- ピアノ協奏曲ト長調* (892478) NEW
- 《ダフニスとクロエ》第 2 組曲* (892471)
- 組曲《マ・メール・ロワ》〔前奏曲と紡ぎ車の踊りを含む〕* (892474)
- 亡き王女のためのパヴァーヌ* (892476)
- スペイン狂詩曲* (892475)
- 組曲〈クープランの墓〉* (892477) NEW
- ラ・ヴァルス* (892473)

リムスキー＝コルサコフ　RIMSKY-KORSAKOV, Nicolai
- スペイン奇想曲 作品 34 (892452)
- 交響組曲「シェエラザード」作品 35* (897151) NEW

レスピーギ　RESPIGHI, Ottorino
- 交響詩「ローマの噴水」* (892484)
- 交響詩「ローマの松」* (892482)
- 交響詩「ローマの祭」* (892483)
- リュートのための古風な舞曲とアリア 第 1, 2, 3 組曲* (892485)
- 組曲《シバの女王ベルキス》* (892481)

ロッシーニ　ROSSINI, Gioachino
- 《セヴィリアの理髪師》序曲 (890752)
- 《ウィリアム・テル》序曲 (890751)

サン＝サーンス　SAINT-SAËNS, Camille
- 交響曲第 3 番ハ短調 作品 78「オルガン」* (897231) NEW
- 動物の謝肉祭* (897232) NEW

シューベルト　SCHUBERT, Franz
- 交響曲第7(8)番ロ短調「未完成」* (897141) NEW
- 交響曲第9(7)番ハ長調「ザ・グレート」* (890611) NEW
- ピアノ五重奏曲イ長調 作品 114「鱒（ます）」(890671)

ショスタコーヴィチ　SHOSTAKOVICH, Dmitri
- 交響曲第 1 番ヘ短調 作品 10 (891805)
- 交響曲第 2 番ロ長調 作品 14「10 月革命」(891806)
- 交響曲第 3 番変ホ長調 作品 12「メーデー」(891803)
- 交響曲第 4 番ハ短調 作品 43 (891804)
- 交響曲第 5 番ニ短調 作品 47 (891801)
- 交響曲第 6 番ロ短調 作品 54 (891810)
- 交響曲第 7 番ハ長調 作品 60「レニングラード」(891807)
- 交響曲第 8 番ハ短調 作品 65 (891808)
- 交響曲第 9 番変ホ長調 作品 70 (891809)
- 交響曲第 10 番ホ短調 作品 93 (891802)
- 交響曲第 11 番ト短調 作品 103「1905 年」(891811)
- 交響曲第 12 番ニ短調 作品 112「1917 年」(891812)
- 交響曲第 13 番変ロ短調 作品 113「バビ・ヤール」(891813)
- 交響曲第 14 番ト短調 作品 135「死者の歌」(891814)
- 交響曲第 15 番イ長調 作品 141 (891815)
- バレエ組曲《ボルト》作品 27a（バレエ組曲第 5 番）*◆ (891822)
- 祝典序曲 作品 96 (891820)
- 映画音楽《ハムレット》作品 116 (15 曲) *◆ (891824)
- 《ホヴァンシチナ》前奏曲（編曲）→ムソルグスキー参照 (892252)
- 〈タヒチ・トロット〉作品 16／ジャズ組曲第 1 番*◆ (897351) NEW
- ステージ・オーケストラのための組曲 [ジャズ組曲第 2 番]*◆ (891823)
- ピアノ協奏曲第 1 番ハ短調 作品 35 (891845)
- ピアノ協奏曲第 2 番ヘ長調 作品 102 (891846)
- ヴァイオリン協奏曲第 1 番イ短調 作品 77 (891843)
- ヴァイオリン協奏曲第 2 番嬰ハ短調 作品 129 (891844)
- チェロ協奏曲第 1 番変ホ長調 作品 107 (891841)
- チェロ協奏曲第 2 番ト短調 作品 126 (891842)
- 弦楽四重奏曲集〔合本〕：
  - 第 1 巻 (第 1 番 作品 49；第 2 番 作品 68；第 3 番 作品 73) (891851)
  - 第 2 巻 (第 4 番 作品 83；第 5 番 作品 92；第 6 番 作品 101) (891852)
  - 第 3 巻 (第 7 番 作品 108；第 8 番 作品 110；第 9 番 作品 117) (891853)
  - 第 4 巻 (第 10 番 作品 118；第 11 番 作品 122；第 12 番 作品 133) (891854)
  - 第 5 巻 (第 13 番 作品 138；第 14 番 作品 142；第 15 番 作品 144) (891855)
- 未完成の弦楽四重奏曲〔第 9 番 初期稿 (1962 年)〕* (891856)
- オラトリオ《森の歌》作品 81*[ロシア語歌詞対訳付] (891861)

シベリウス　SIBELIUS, Jean
- 交響曲第 2 番ニ長調 作品 43* (892522)
- 交響曲第 5 番変ホ長調 作品 82* (892523)
- 交響詩「フィンランディア」作品 26* (892521)
- 「カレリア」組曲 作品 11* (892524)
- ヴァイオリン協奏曲ニ短調 作品 47* (892525)

スメタナ　SMETANA, Bedřich
- 交響詩「モルダウ（ヴルタヴァ）」* (897161)

シュトラウス、リヒャルト　STRAUSS, Richard
- 〈サロメの踊り〉* (891731) NEW

チャイコフスキー　TCHAIKOVSKY, Peter
- 交響曲第 1 番ト短調 作品 13「冬の日の幻想」* (891621)
- 交響曲第 4 番ヘ短調 作品 36* (897121) NEW
- 交響曲第 5 番ホ短調 作品 64* (897122) NEW
- 交響曲第 6 番ロ短調 作品 74「悲愴」* (897123) NEW
- スラヴ行進曲 作品 31* (897125) NEW
- イタリア奇想曲 作品 45* (891616)
- 荘厳序曲「1812 年」作品 49* (897126) NEW
- 幻想序曲「ロメオとジュリエット」* (891615)
- 弦楽セレナーデ ハ長調 作品 48* (897124) NEW
- バレエ組曲《白鳥の湖》作品 20〔抜粋：10 曲〕* (891613)
- 組曲《眠れる森の美女》作品 66a* (891612)
- 組曲《くるみ割り人形》作品 71a* (891611)
- ピアノ協奏曲第 1 番変ロ短調 作品 23* (897128) NEW
- ヴァイオリン協奏曲ニ長調 作品 35* (897127) NEW
- 弦楽四重奏曲第 1 番ニ長調 作品 11（「アンダンテ・カンタービレ」）(891671)

外山雄三　TOYAMA, Yuzo
- 管弦楽のためのラプソディ*[改訂版] (893650)

ヴェルディ　VERDI, Giuseppe
- 《シチリア島の夕べの祈り》序曲 (890781) NEW

ヴィヴァルディ　VIVALDI, Antonio
- 協奏曲集「四季」作品 8，1－4 (890141)
- フルート協奏曲ヘ長調 作品 10-1「海の嵐」(890142)

ワーグナー　WAGNER, Richard
- 《さまよえるオランダ人》（さすらいのオランダ人）序曲 (892356)
- 《ローエングリン》- 第 I, III 幕への前奏曲/エルザの大聖堂への入場 (897216) NEW
- 《ニュルンベルクのマイスタージンガー》- 第 I 幕への前奏曲* (897211) NEW
- 《パルジファル》- 前奏曲と聖金曜日の音楽* (897212) NEW
- ジークフリート牧歌* (897215) NEW
- 《タンホイザー》序曲 [ドレスデン版]* (897213) NEW
- 《トリスタンとイゾルデ》- 前奏曲と愛の死* (897214) NEW
- ヴァルキューレの騎行（《ヴァルキューレ》- 第 III 幕への前奏曲）(892353)

ウェーバー　WEBER, Carl Maria von
- 《魔弾の射手》序曲 (892751)